MIKE PENCE

EQUALLY YOKED BY GRACE

WRITTEN BY
Alfred Stephen Kanu

ISBN 978-1-0980-0426-2 (paperback)
ISBN 978-1-0980-0428-6 (digital)

Copyright © 2019 by Alfred Stephen Kanu

All rights reserved. No part of this publication may be reproduced, distributed, or transmitted in any form or by any means, including photocopying, recording, or other electronic or mechanical methods without the prior written permission of the publisher. For permission requests, solicit the publisher via the address below.

Christian Faith Publishing, Inc.
832 Park Avenue
Meadville, PA 16335
www.christianfaithpublishing.com

Printed in the United States of America

I'd like to dedicate this book to my lovely family. First to my beautiful wife, Jennifer Kanu. Next to my firstborn, Alexander Kanu, and my lovely princess and daughter Abigail Kanu. Last but not the least, to my third son, Alfred Jr.

I started writing this book when he was in his mother's womb. I thought I'd finish writing before he was born, but all things work out together for good.

I would like to recognize few more people that are important to me My brother Alpha Kanu and wife Coral, also my pastor and Wife who has being my spiritual mentor Pastor Abayomi Ajibola and wife Folakeh Ajibola.

Also, this is for all conservatives and well-mannered *deplorable* who voted to bring a real change to America during the 2016 election year.

Finally to Vice President Mike Pence and his family for being role models as to how leaders should lead and conduct themselves—with humility and dignity.

PREFACE

This book, according to its title, is about our current vice president, Mike Pence. Why in the world did I, as a first-time writer or author, choose to write about the vice president? I decided to take this adventure as a launching pad for my writing career even though a professional writer will not advise me to take on a very high-profile figure to write about.

When I thought about it myself, I think it was a big risk. I remember the evening I called my wife and told her that I was going to write a book and it's going to be about our current vice president. You know what she said? "Why not write about yourself?"

I told her, "Baby, I will write about myself later." I also told her it is very important for me to do it now because the past presidential election in 2016 has opened a lot of topics and writing opportunities. And most of you will be wondering why I chose former governor and now vice president Mike Pence as my main subject.

The reason being that he helps give hope to America again on a conservative perspective as a Christian first and then as vice president. And as I stated earlier, I am a practicing Christian myself. It is a great honor to write about Vice President Mike Pence. His journey to the second highest level of office in the United States of America amazes me and is very inspiring to me personally, and I do believe it means a lot to the conservatives and also within evangelical community to have someone second-in-command as a vice president who stands for principles left behind by the founding fathers and support religious liberty.

He is one of the individuals who helped make this election a historic event. During this writing, I will be diving deeper on his journey to this new position he now holds—Vice President of the

United States—and his challenges and obstacles. Most of all, the great leap of faith he took in answering to the call of then candidate-elect Donald Trump to be his vice and running mate on the campaign trail.

CHAPTER 1

Who Is Mike Pence?

According to public records, the biography of Vice President Mike Pence is recorded as born and raised in Columbus, Indiana. His full name is Michael Richard Mike Pence who was born on June 7, 1959, as one of the six children by his mother, Nancy Jane Cowley, and Edward J. Pence Jr. who passed away in 1988 (may his soul rest in peace). His dad was a businessman who migrated from Ireland to the United States and became a bus driver in Chicago, Illinois.

Mike Pence attended Columbus North High School in 1977 where he graduated, and he also studied history at Hanover College in 1981. He furthered his study at Indiana University where he studied law at Robert H. McKinney School of Law in 1986.

After graduating from Hanover, Mike Pence was admissions counselor at the college from 1981 to 1983. His religious background as a young man was Roman Catholic, and he was a Democrat by political affiliation. He also started out as a volunteer for the Bartholomew County Democratic party in 1976 and voted for Jimmy Carter in the 1980 presidential election. His aspiration for politics started at an early age and was inspired by people such as John F. Kennedy and Martin Luther King Jr.

Mike Pence became an evangelical born-again Christian. Soon after that, he began to have a shift in his political views lining toward the right-wing ideology sometimes which Mike Pence attribute to "common sense conservatism of Ronald Reagan that began to identify with."

After his graduation from law school in 1986, he was an attorney in private practice. He also ran unsuccessfully for congressional seat in 1988. Mike Pence became the president of the Indiana Policy Review Foundation, a self-described free market think tank in 1990. In 1991, he also became a member of the State Policy Network.

In 1993, Mike Pence left the Indiana Policy Review Foundation a year after beginning to host *The Mike Pence Show*, a talk-radio program based in WRCR-FM in Rushville, Indiana. "He called himself *Rush Limbaugh on decaf* because he sees himself politically conservative while not outspoken as Limbaugh. The show was syndicated in Network Indiana and aired on weekdays from 9:00 a.m. to noon (ET) on eighteen stations throughout the state including WIBC in Indianapolis. All credits to Wikipedia for biography outline.

While going through his biography, I saw someone who is determined and ready to serve relentlessly from one capacity to the other no matter the huddles or obstacles that comes his way. I see a fighter and an achiever who is determined to serve as a civil servant dedicated to public service and country. That is very inspiring to me.

In life, nothing comes easy. The amount of perseverance and effort Mike Pence put in to get to where he is now is *huge*, our then candidate Donald Trump said. When he loses two bids for a US congressional seat in 1988, he never gave up which, I believe, at that time was due to the fact that he was very new to the political arena as a fresher, trying to break out in this vast political field in America. Whether it is a run for a city mayor or president, there is a lot of politics involved, especially if you don't have the political machine behind you.

After that attempt, he retreated into running a conservative radio talk and television talk show where he gained lots of audience, and that became his launching pad and platform for all his future political adventures. To enter the stage of politics, you don't just graduate from law school and think the career-long politicians will let you ride easy. But introducing yourself to a wider audience will allow them to know who you are, what you stand for, and what your values and beliefs systems are.

I believe Mike Pence demonstrated all that including his love for America and his patriotic commitment in serving the people—whether in Indiana or the country as a whole. After spending time in the media world, Mike Pence ran again for office in 2000 as a representative congressman for the State of Indiana at the United States House of Representatives where he served from 2001 to 2013 and was the chairman of the House Republican Conference from 2009 to 2011.

I don't know how far back his leadership calling came from, but according to his college biography, he has been championing leadership role for the longest. When you are endowed with leadership gift and skill, you will become a hero to many no wonder that for any position he took, he must be a leader in that particular capacity, which is awesome. I want to call him born to lead. How can someone be a leader? You must have skills in dealing with people and the ability to bring people together. I really admire his calm personality even in difficult situations which is an excellent quality of a leader.

He worked as a US congressman and represented Indiana's second congressional district which was renumbered as the sixth district later on. Mike Pence is a conservative Christian and is publicly known for his Christian belief and is not ashamed of it.

As Christ say in the Bible, "If you're ashamed of me in front of men, I will be ashamed of you in front of my father in heaven." He is also part of the Tea Party movement which includes hard-core Republican members with conservative views of running the government or how the United States government must operate. For example, smart budgeting, government spending, and limited government. They also favor lower taxes. They are lovers of the American Constitution, especially the 2nd Amendment, the right to bear arm engrave in the Constitution by the founding fathers for Americans to be able to protect and defend themselves against individual and in case of government suppression on its citizens.

In his first year in office, Mike Pence gained recognition as one with strong conviction, always willing to his own way. He was one of the congressmen who opposed the former president George W. Bush when he introduced the No Child Left Behind Act back in 2001. He also opposed President Bush's Medicare prescription drug expansion. In 2006, Mike Pence was elected again in the house election where he defeated Democrat Barry Welsh. Because of his outstanding performance in the Republican Party, he began to move up in ranking. He was chairman of the Republican study committee which involved a group of conservative House Republicans. He also announced his candidacy for leader of the Republican Party minority leader in the United States House of Representatives.

He ran on the idea of "returning to the values of the Newt Gingrich headed 1994 Republican Revolution." He did lose his bid to representative John Boehner of Ohio by vote 168 for John Boehner and Mike Pence, 27. Wow, that was a landslide win. Was it because of strong stance as conservative? Or maybe Boehner has been waiting in line for that position.

As you can see, twenty-seven may only be from a few Tea Party members who backed him, but again, what I see as pattern for Mike Pence is this: one loss of opportunity creates another for him. He went on to became the Republican conference chairman, which is third highest-ranking Republican leadership position. He ran unopposed and was elected overwhelmingly, and that makes him the first to hold that position from Indiana States. I see him as a man of opportunity. When one shuts, another opens for him, and he is not afraid to enter in and make the most out every office he holds.

CHAPTER 2

Mike Pence as Former Governor

Mike Pence was a former governor for the State of Indiana, a position of which he let go of in 2016 then ran as a running mate with candidate Trump. Now he is the 45th Vice President of the United States of America. In May of 2011, he announced that he would be seeking the Republican nomination for governor of the state of Indiana in 2012.

The incumbent Republican at that time was Governor Mitch Daniels. Despite a strong name recognition and popularity of the outgoing governor of the same party, Mike Pence had heated race but ended up winning with just under 50 percent of the vote against Democrat John R. Gregg and Libertarian nominee Rupert Boneham.

Mike Pence retained his victory and was sworn in on January 14, 2013 as the 50th Governor of Indiana. During his work as a governor, Mike Pence inherited a $2-billion budget reserved from his predecessor, Mitch Daniels, and the state added to that reserve under his watch not before requiring state agencies, including the public universities to reduce funding in years in which revenue fell below the projections.

The state finished fiscal year 2014 with a reserve of $2 billion. Budget cuts ordered by Mike Pence for $14 billion annual state budget include $24 million cut from colleges and universities and $27 million cut from family and social service administration. He also did a $12-million cut from the department of correction. The then governor made some drastic cut to his state expenses using conservative's common sense principles.

Indiana has one of the lowest corporate taxes in the country in his time as a governor in order to encourage job growth from the private sector. He tried to cut the income tax rate to 10 percent but was unsuccessful. On June 12, 2013, the Indiana Legislature overrode Mike Pence's veto of a bill to retroactively authorize a local tax. Lawmakers overrode his veto in a 68–23 vote in the House and a 34–12 one in the Senate. Members of his own party overwhelmingly voted against Pence, but he was supported by most Democrats.

He also vetoed the Jackson Pulaski tax fix, one of three bills vetoed by the governor. Mike Pence also addresses a fifteen-year-old county income tax which was imposed to fund the construction of jail facilities with the hope that the tax be lowered by 1 percent after the first few years. This reduction was not implemented; and thus, county resident paid an additional 1 percent tax that were legally not required to pay the bill pass with huge majority but was later vetoed by Mike Pence and allowed money to be kept and not return to taxpayers as would have otherwise be necessary.

The former governor pushes hard to maintain a balance budget and an amendment to the state's constitution. He had initially proposed the initiative in his state at the State Address in January 2015. The legislation passed and the State Senate. Because of their determination to manage their budget well, the State of Indiana has had AAA credit ratings with the three major credit-rating agencies since 2010 before Mike Pence took over and the ratings has been maintained throughout his time in office.

In 2014, Mike Pence supported the Indiana Gateway project, a $71.4 million passenger-and-freight rail improvement initiative paid for by the American Recovery and Reinvestment Act of 2009, which was a Federal stimulus package which he voted against while he was a congressman. In October 2015, he "announced plans to pay of $250 million federal loan" to cover unemployment insurance payments that spiked during the recession.

Mike Pence signed legislation to fund a $230 million two-year road funding package. As our current vice president, Americans are expecting him to apply his wisdom together with current President Donald J. Trump to tackle the almost $20 trillion debt of the United States owed to foreign government using strict conservatives budget principle in reducing the national debt which, I believe, this administration is already working on.

Mike Pence, on education during his time as governor, supported significant increases in education funding to preschools, voucher programs, and charter schools but frequently clashed with supporters of traditional public school. In 2014, a little over one year after taking office, Mike Pence helped establish a $10 million state preschool pilot program in the State of Indiana and testified personally before the state Senate Education committee in favor of the program to convince fellow Republican of which several opposed the proposal to approve the plan.

Although the plan was defeated, Mike Pence successfully managed to revive it, getting Indiana off the list of just ten states that spent no direct fund to help the poor children attend preschool. Mike Pence spent more resources in promoting education in Pre-K Program without federal interference. After coming under sustained criticism for his position, he reversed his course and sought to apply for the funds.

In 2015, Mike Pence secured significant increases in charter school funding from legislation although he did not get everything he had proposed. The legislation was signed into law by Mike Pence in 2013, which greatly increased the number of students in Indiana who qualified for school vouchers, making it one of the largest voucher programs in the United States. The annual cost of the program is estimated to $53 million in school year 2015 through 2016.

Mike Pence also opposed the common core standards initiative, calling for a full repeal of the standards in his 2014 State of the State address. The Indiana General Assembly then passed a bill to repeal the standards becoming the first state to do so. Despite successful advocacy for more funding for preschools, voucher programs, and charter schools, Mike pence has frequently clashed with teachers' unions and supporters of public schooling.

In one of his first acts as governor, Mike Pence removed control of Educational Employment Relations Board, which was in charge of handling conflicts between unions and school boards. Pence created a new center for Education and Career Innovation (CECI) to coordinate efforts between schools and private sector. He was highly criticized by Glenda Ritz, a Democrat who stated that it was a *power grab* and an encroachment on her own duties. Mike Pence eventually disestablished the center in order to help defuse the conflict. In May of 2015, Mike Pence signed a bill stripping Ritz of much of her authority over standardized testing and other education issues and reconstituting the state board of education dominated by Pence's appointees. The bill also allowed the board to appoint a chairman other than the superintendent of public instruction starting in 2017 and added the state board of education controlled by Pence as a state educational authority along with the departments of education (controlled by Ritz) for purposes of accessing sensitive student data. Mike Pence and Ritz also clashed over non-binding federal guidelines that advised Indiana public schools to treat transgender student in a way that corresponds to their gender identity, even if their education files indicate a different gender.

Mike Pence Energy Policy and the Environment

During Pence's term in office, the republican-controlled Indiana General Assembly repeatedly tried to roll back the renewable energy standards and successfully ended Indian's energy efficiency efforts. Mike Pence has been an outspoken supporter of the coal industry, declaring in his 2015 State Address that Indiana is pro-coal state, which he expressed support for an above energy strategy, stating that "we must continue to oppose President Obama denouncing the EPA'S clean power plan," which would have regulate carbon emission from existing power plans and stating that Indiana refused to comply with the plan. Indian joined other states in a lawsuit seeking to invalidate the plan. Mike Pence stated that even if the legal challenges failed, Indiana would continue to defy the rule and would not come up with its own plan to reduce emissions.

His Gun Policy

In 2014, over the opposition of Indiana school organizations, Mike Pence signed a bill which allows firearms to be kept in vehicles on school property. In 2015, following the shooting in Chattanooga, Mike Pence recruited the NRA to train the Indiana National Guard on concealed carry. Some National Guard officials from other states question why a civilian organization would be involved in a military issue.

In May 2015, Mike Pence signed Senate Bill 98 into law, which limited against gun manufacturers and retailers that allegedly made illegal sales of handguns. The bill was supported by Republicans such as Jim Tomes, who hoped that the measure would attract more gun-related businesses to Indiana but was opposed by Gary mayor and former Indiana Attorney General Keren Freeman-Wilson, who viewed the measure as an unprecedented violation of the separation of powers between the legislative and judicial branches of state government. In 2016, Pence signed Senate Bill 109 into law, legalizing the captive hunting of farm-raised deer in Indiana.

The Governors Work on Public Health Issues

In the beginning of December 2014, there was an HIV outbreak in Southern Indiana. In 2011, Planned Parenthood ran five rural clinics in Indiana where they offered HIV test and other prevention and early intervention which includes counseling for better health. The plan parent facility in Scott County did not perform any abortions.

The Republican-controlled legislature and Governor Pence defunded Planned Parenthood. Scott County has been without an HIV testing center since 2013. Mike Pence had long been a vocal opponent of needle exchange programs, which allow drug users to trade in used syringes for sterile ones in order to stop the spread of the diseases despite evidence that such programs prevent the spread of AIDS and hepatitis C and do not increase drug abuse.

In March 2015, after the outbreak began, Mike Pence allowed at least five counties to open needle exchanges but has not moved to lift the state ban on funding for the needle exchanges. Even though critics say Mike Pence's compromises has been ineffective because counties had no way to pay for needle exchanges themselves, Indiana State Health Commissioner Jerome Adams defended Mike Pence, saying that publicly funded needle exchange programs are controversial in many conservative communities.

In Middle America, Adams said, "You can't just point your finger at folks and say, 'You need to have a syringe exchange, and we're going to pay for it with your tax dollars.'" In 2015, the Obama administration agreed to expand Medicaid in Indian in accordance with the Affordable Care Act.

CHAPTER 3

Religion and LGBT Rights Controversies

Governor Mike Pence was successful on many policies he initiates. The former governor faces several high-profile controversies, including some that brought national attention. On March 26, 2015, Mike Pence signed the Indiana Senate Bill 101, also known as the Indiana *religious objection bill* (Religious Freedom Restoration Act or RFRA) into laws.

The law signing was met with criticism by people and groups who felt the law was carefully worded in a way that would permit discrimination against LGBT persons. Such organization as the NCAA, the gamer convention Gen Con, and the Disciples of Christ spoke out against the law. Apple CEO Tim Cook and Saleforce.com CEO Marc Benioff condemned the law with saleforce.com saying it would halt its plans to expand in the state. Angie's list announced that they will cancel $40 million expansion of their Indianapolis-based headquarters due to concerns over the law. The expansion would have moved one thousand jobs into the state. The mayors of San Francisco and Seattle banned official traveling to Indiana. Thousand protested against the policy.

Five GOP state representatives voted against the bill, and Greg Ballard, the Republican mayor of Indianapolis, criticized it as sending the wrong signal about the state. Governor Mike Pence defended the law, stating that it was not about discrimination. In an appearance on ABC News program with George Stephanopoulos, the then governor stated that "we are not going to change the law" while refusing to answer whether examples of discrimination against LGBT people given by Eric Miller of anti-LGBT group Advance America would be legal under the law.

Mike Pence denied that the law permitted discrimination and wrote in a March 31, 2015 *Wall Street Journal* op-ed, "If I saw a restaurant owner refuse to serve a gay couple, I wouldn't eat there anymore. As governor of Indiana, if I were presented a bill that legalized discrimination against any person or group, I would veto it."

In the wake of the backlash against the RFRA, on April 2, 2015, Governor Pence signed legislation revising the law to prevent potential discrimination. (Courtesy of Wikipedia public Record). As a conservative, Governor Mike Pence knows the era at which we are living in America where those who do not participate in the LGBT movement have been harassed to perform duties that goes against their religious values, and if you fail to perform such task, they will come down heavily on you. Just as we see all the big names going against the governor and his state, we have also witnessed a court clerk being thrown into jail for not performing a gay wedding due to her religious conviction. Whether they were trying their approach of harassment on non-conformers, they were met with huge critics by people of conservatives value. At least somebody have to fight for those that hold on to deep religious practice. Also, thanks to the founding fathers for their wisdom in providing freedom of religion without being shut down by others labeling people with unnecessary name-calling.

Abortion Controversy

Another controversy arose in March 2016 when Mike Pence signed into law H.B.1337, a bill that both banned certain abortion procedures and placed new restriction on abortion providers. The bill banned abortion if the reason for the procedures given by the pregnant person was the fetus race or gender or a fetal abnormality.

In addition, it required that all the fetal remains from abortions or miscarriages at any stage of pregnancy be buried or cremated which, according to the Guttmacher Institute, was not required in any other state. It was described as "exceptional for its breath." If implemented, it would have Indiana the first state to have a blanket ban on abortions based solely on race, sex, or suspected disabilities, including evidence of down syndrome.

Days after the US Supreme decision in Whole Women's Health v. Hellerstedt, a federal court issued a preliminary injunction blocking the bill from taking effect, with US district judge Tanya Walton Pratt determining that the bill was likely to be unconstitutional and that the state of Indiana would be unlikely to prevail at trial. Mike Pence announced on January 25, 2017, that he would speak at 2017 March for life, a first for any vice president. (Courtesy of Wikipedia public record)

Governor Mike Pence is a man with purpose and with a deep conscience. The things that the creator will care about his Christian belief have shaped his way of governing in every area of his of life. It is sad that we find our self in a falling world where group of people will forsake those good morals that will make humanity better. Also, what most conservatives care about when it comes to living our lives in morally defined way, to many, is considered radical living—and many people are not ready to go down that path.

The Western civilization has embrace secularism and humanism, which in such system to govern with sound moral values has become a battleground for legal intervention of higher court system. In the various policies, what the former governor tries to implement are very controversial in the era we live in. One thing am encouraged by Mike Pence is he always believes in doing what is right no matter the attacks he received. We have seen that time and time again.

I admire his governing style which shows that after doing what is right, you only owe obligation to one person which is your creator because only you alone will stand before him on judgment day, which most politicians don't take into consideration: all people in power and in authority will stand before the one who has all powers in both heaven on earth. But the choice is up to us. You can rule in righteousness or rule in corruption. Everyone will stand before him and give an account one day. Did you care about the things God care about, or are you a people pleaser filled with political correctness?

The Controversy with the Media and the Press

In June 2013, Governor Mike Pence was criticized for deleting others' comment that were posted on his official government Facebook page, which he apologized for. On January 26, 2015, it was widely reported that Mike Pence had planned to lunch state-run taxpayer funded news service for Indiana. The service will be called JustIN, and the two employees who would run it were to be overseen by former reporter for the *Indianapolis Star* and would feature breaking news, stories written by press secretaries, and light features.

At the time, it was reported that the two employees who would run the news service would be paid a combined $100,000 yearly salary. The target audience was small newspapers that had limited staff, but the site would also serve to communicate directly with public. The publisher of the *Commercial Review* of Portland, Indiana, said, "I think it's a ludicrous idea the notion of elected official presenting material that will inevitably have pro-administration point of view is antithetical to the idea of independent press. There was speculation that the news service would publish pro-administration stories that would make Mike Pence look good in event of presidential run."

According to the Associated Press, the idea "of stories prewritten for the media set off a wave of criticism from journalists around the country who likened the Indiana endeavor to state-run media in Russia and China. Headlines like "Pravda On The Plains" accompanied call for Mike Pence to scrap the idea. David A. Graham of the *Atlantic* regarded the announcement of justIN as evidence of a disturbing, changing trend in how the public gets news.

After a week or so of controversy about the idea, Mike Pence scrapped the idea saying, "However well intentioned, after thorough review of the preliminary planning and careful consideration of the concerns expressed, I am writing you to inform you that I have made a decision to terminate development of justIN website immediately" (Courtesy of Wikipedia public record).

This is not the only time the governor has back out of a propose idea or project he intend to carry out. He has always been faced with wide array of criticism and condemnation by either the media and/or objecting individual within the Indiana legislators.

Writing the book has made me know him even the more. One thing I realized about Mike Pence is his courage to pull through challengers and obstacles. I do believe it was a training ground for a bigger purpose and better future that his critics and oppositions will never achieve. As the saying goes, what doesn't kill you makes you stronger—that goes for our Vice President Mike Pence.

The Syrian Refugee Crisis

As governor, Mike Pence attempted unsuccessfully to prevent Syrian refugees from being resettled in Indiana. In February 2016, a federal judge ruled that Pence's cut of federal funds for local non-profit refugee resettlement agency was unconstitutional; Mike Pence appealed. In December 2015, Mike Pence stated that calls to ban Muslims from entering the US was offensive and are unconstitutional.

On the Theory of Evolution

When asked if he accepts evolution, Mike Pence answered, "I believe with all my heart that God created the heavens and the earth, the seas, and all that's in them. How he did that, I'll ask him about that someday."

In a 2002 statement on the floor of the house (reported in congressional record), Mike Pence told his colleagues, "I also believe that someday, scientists will come to see that only the intelligent design provides even a remotely rational explanation for the known universe" (courtesy of Wikipedia).

If you are a Christian and someone conservative in government office, get ready for all the scrutiny and unusual question just because your belief is all coming from a left-wing progressive wing who have voted out the creator from their lives, and so they think everyone is like them in terms of their firm, believing in evolution and other theories that exclude the mentioning of a sovereign God. By asking someone like Mike Pence about the evolution theory, they should expect no other answer than mentioning God the creator of the heavens and the earth. If a Christian says otherwise, it is like denying your God because those are fundamental doctrines of the Christian faith. Rejecting all other doctrine is meaningless.

Reelection Campaign and Withdrawal

Governor Mike Pence ran for a second term as governor. He was unopposed in May 3, 2016, Republican Primary for governor. He was to face Democrat John R. Gregg, former speaker of the Indiana House of Representatives, in rematch of the 2012 race. However, Pence filed paperwork ending his campaign on July 15, 2016, as Trump announced his selection of Mike Pence as his vice presidential running mate.

Credits to Wikipedia for the brief biography of the former Governor Mike Pence—his tenure in office as governor, his life story, place of birth, early years before college, and up to his last days as governor.

CHAPTER 4

On Immigration

In June 2006, Mike Pence unveiled an immigration plan which he described as "No Amnesty Immigration reform" that would include increased border security, followed by strict enforcement of laws against hiring illegal aliens, and guest worker program. This guest worker program would have required participants to apply from their home country to government approve job placement agencies that match workers with employer who cannot find Americans for the job. The plan received support from conservative such as Dick Armey but attracted criticism from other conservatives such as Richard Viguerie and Phyllis Schlafly and Pat Buchanan, who as described by the New York Times, collectively viewed Mike Pence as lending "conservative prestige to form of liberal amnesty. In 2009, Mike Pence opposed birthright citizenship (the legal principle set forth by the Citizenship Clause of the Fourteenth Amendment to the United States Constitution that "All persons born or naturalized in the United States, and subjected to jurisdiction thereof, are citizens the United State and of the State wherein they reside"). He co-sponsored a bill that would have limited citizenship to children born to at least one percent who is a citizen, immigrants living permanently in the U.S or non- citizens performing active service in the Armed Forces. In 2010, Mike Pence voted against the Dream Act, which would grant the undocumented children of illegal immigrants' conditional non-immigrant status if they met certain requirements. He also stated in 2010 that Arizona S.B. 1070. Which at the time of passage in 2010 was the nation's broadest and strictest anti-illegal immigration legislation, was a good faith to try and restore order to their communities.

Mike Pence on Social Security

Mr Pence supported president George W. Bush unsuccessful 2005 proposal to partially privatize Social Security by allowing workers to invest part of their Social Security payroll taxes in private investment account and reduce the increase in benefits for high-income participants. Mr Pence had previously proposed a similar bill but more aggressive reform plan than president Bush's. When he was asked in 2010 if he would be willing to make a cut to Social Security, Mr. Pence answered, I think everything has to be on the table. When asked if he would raise the retirement age, he said, "I'm an all of the above guy. We need to look at everything on the menu.

The Patriot Act

Mr. Pence supported the Patriot Act on its passage in 2001, and in 2005 called the act "essential to our continued success in war on terror here at home. Mr. Pence was sponsor of the legislation in 2009 to extend three expiring provision of the Patriot Act (library records provision, the roving -wiretap provision, and the lone-wolf provision) for an additional ten years.

International Trade

Mr. Pence "has been a longtime aggressive advocate of trade deals" between the U.S and foreign countries. He has been supporter of the North American Free Trade Agreement (NAFTA), and during his tenure in the House, he voted for every free- trade agreement that came before him. Mr. Pence voted in favor of the Central American Free Trade Agreement (CAFTA); in favor of keeping the U.S in the world Trade Organization; and in favor of permanent normal trade with China. Mr. Pence also supported bilateral free -trade agreements with Colombia, South Korea, Panama, Peru, Oman, Chile and Singapore. Pence strong stance in favor of free trade sharply differs from the stance of his running mate Trump, who has condemned globalization and the liberalization of trade. Mr Pence voted against the Trade and globalization Act of 2007, which would have expanded Trade Adjustment Assistance to American workers adversely affected by globalization. However, in 2014 Mr. Pence called for the "swift adoption" of the Trans-Pacific Partnership (TPP), urging Indiana's congressional delegation to support the trade deal.

Foreign Policy

Mr. Pence Supported the Iraq War Resolution, which authorized military action against Iraq. During the Iraq war Mr. Pence opposes setting a public withdrawal date from Iraq. During an April 2007 visit to Baghdad, Pence and John McCain visited Sharjah market, the site of deadly attack in February of 2007, that claimed the lives of sixty-one people. Mr. Pence and John McCain described the visit as evidence that the security situation in Iraqi markets had improved. The visit to the market took place under tight security, including helicopters overhead, and the New York Times reported that the visit gave false indication of how secure the area was because of the extremely heavy security forces use to protect them. Mr. Pence chaired the House Foreign Affairs Subcommittee on the Middle East and was a prominent supporter of George W. Bush's Iraq War troop surge of 2007. At the time, Mr. Pence stated that the surge is working and defending the initial decision to invade in 2003. He also opposed closing the Guantanamo Bay detention camp and trying the suspected terrorist in the United States. As an alternative, Mr. Pence has said that the "enemy combatants" should be tried in a military tribunal. He has also stated his support for Israel and its right to attack facilities in Iran to prevent the Iranians from developing nuclear weapons, has defended the actions of Israel in its use of deadly force in enforcing blockage of Gaza, and has referred to Israel as "America's cherished ally". He visited Israel in 2014 to express his support, and in 2016 signed into law a bill which would ban Indiana from having any commercial dealings with a company that boycott Israel. He opposed a Palestinian State. Mr. Pence criticized Russian president Vladimir Putin and Barack Obama's alleged weak leadership, saying "When Donald Trump and I observe that, as I've said in the Syria, in Iran, in Ukraine, that the small and bullying leader of Russia has been stronger on the world stage than this administration, that stating painful facts. That's not an endorsement of Vladimir Putin. That's an indictment of weak and feckless leadership.

When it comes to foreign policy every leader will live with their decision on matters related to other countries their way of governance and leadership Mr. Pence supported the removal of former Libyan President Gaddafi.

Crime and illegal drugs

Mr. Pence has questioned proposals to decrease penalties for low level marijuana offenses in Indiana, saying that the state should focus on "reducing crime, not reducing penalties. In 2013 Mr. Pence expressed concern that a then – pending bill to revise the state's criminal code was not tough enough on drug crimes, and successfully lobbied to limit the reduction in sentencing of marijuana offences.

In 2016 he signed into law a measure that would reinstate a ten-year mandatory minimum prison sentence for certain drug offenders. In 2014, Pence sent a letter to United State Attorney General Eric Holder, saying that Indiana would not comply with the federal prison rape elimination standards because they were "too expensive". According to the Indiana Department of Corrections, it would cost the state $15-20 million annually to comply been "implemented". In 2015, Mr Pence signed Senate bill 94 to lengthen the statute of limitation for rape continuing for five years after sufficient DNA evidence is uncovered, enough recorded evidence is brought forth or discovered, or the offender confess to the crime. He also signed Senate bill 8 to allow the death penalty for beheadings if the victim was alive at the time of the offence.

All credit to **Wikipedia** for the public record of Mr. Pence.

CHAPTER 5

Equally Yoked by Grace

The coming together of then candidate Trump and Mike Pence, I saw it as a divine connection of which both individual has two different background and personality. During the selection of Donald Trump as the presidential nominee for the national Republican Party, a lot of people did not see that coming even with the well-known names of his running mate who have been prepping themselves for years for a shot at the presidency could not see light at the end of the tunnel. Some popular names like former Texas Governor Jeb Bush's brother to former president George W. Bush, a well-known Republican, former governor Mike Huckabee, Rick Perry, and Governor Chris Christie of New Jersey were in the list of experienced governors who are acquainted or at least have some knowledge about legislative process or leadership role from various state governorship. Even some congressional and Senate members could not pull it off, except for a New York businessman Donald A. Trump.

He became very attractive to the regular or everyday American who, in his way of talking, did not hold back on nothing, was bold and brave like a lion, and sounded like the regular American who speak the language they understand, such as the economy, and security for the American people. Immigration and border control and also healthcare were the issues that the everyday American were facing, and Trump was killing it on each one of these topic including his favorite slogan of "Draining the swamp" and "Make America Great

Again" which became the two popular slogan of 2016–2017 even though the American people have seen the swamp fighting back on all angles.

I found the merger of Donald Trump and Mike Pence as a violation of God's standard. It was joining someone who is almost left lining because finding a conservative from a big liberal city like New York City is very hard to come by and a former governor whose entire life has been pursuing a practical conservative principle from his college days to his role as a governor. His policies as governor all spells conservatism.

According to 2 Corinthians 6:14, the Bible warned Christians not to be equally yoked together in unrighteousness because the Christian should be able to stand out and be an example to those struggling with moral values. The coming together of Mike Pence and Donald Trump, I believe, was the only exception which was for a good cause to assist him in the ruling of God's creation in term of moral values. Mike Pence is well-nourished with biblical principles which makes one the weaker vessel, and for Mr. Trump, he has been in Hollywood, TV spotlight and the entertainment industry that are not morally friendly. But the few things I have seen in Donald Trump is work Ethics. He works hard for the things he wants in life. He loves his family, and most of all, he loves America and shows a character of a true patriot as for his moral values during the election campaign. He spoke a little about his faith as Presbyterian Christian, not actually practicing which is not a prerequisite for being a president of the United States as there should be no religious test for a public servant even though many Americans prefer someone with good moral background in order to keep America as the leading example of a country that upholds good moral standards in the world.

Then candidate Trump even showed the people a Bible that was given to him by his mother as a gift. Because of his other qualities, he can be accepted to most Americans as most Americans are looking for someone who loves the country and not a traitor to the United States. Many people, including me, believe Mike Pence will bring a little balance of sound mind into the leadership of the nation and a well-known conservative who knows around the country.

As a steady-minded individual with very good moral standing, Mike Pence's nomination as a vice president brings hope to many that had worried if Donald Trump would have selected someone else that would have caused a McCain and Palin effect on the election. The American people showed up courage with the nomination of Mike Pence which was a very early sign that candidate Trump was up to a good start even though the Clinton machine was looking very scary because of the donor power they have and the backing of famous people from Hollywood, including a sitting president and first lady who were all hitting the campaign trail for Hillary.

Many Republicans and independent began to gain confidence in candidate Trump due to his choice for vice president. I don't really know if the Republican National Committee helped Trump pick the vice president or if it was his personal decision. I know he had some other qualified names on the list of picks, but as I said earlier, Mike Pence was destined to be the vice president for such a time as this. People consider him as the balance in tone at the White House as the president is more of a bombastic speaker who, most of the time, has to restate most of comment in a refined way to prevent backlash.

Answering the Call from Candidate-Elect Trump

I don't think Governor Mike Pence know beforehand that he was going to be the running mate of candidate elect Donald Trump at that time because Mike Pence was busy as governor and was also preparing for gubernatorial election in the State of Indiana. He was going to be campaigning for a second term as governor for the State of Indiana. He was to face Democrat John R. Gregg, former Speaker of the house of the Indiana House of Representatives. I personally admire Mike Pence's dedication to public service which has led him to second highest position in the land since his early political career up to this current position as vice president. I totally admire his consistency, perseverance, and commitment to service. He is a role model public servant even though his conservative principles were usually met with a lot of contentions, but one thing you cannot find in him is giving up. He doesn't give up. I hope young aspiring public servants will learn from him.

Another quality I have learned from Mike Pence in writing this book is his love to serve people as a public servant. It is all about serving people. In all his career, he has been serving people in various leadership role. As of now, he is experiencing one of the highest rewards in being a public servant and a statesman. Going back to Mike Pence's background in his political career, his failures and victories in past have prepared him for this office. His faith and conservative values go together with him everywhere he goes of which he is not ashamed of and is very bold about it.

I remember when Mike Pence introduced himself first as Christian; second, a conservative; and third, a Republican. In that order, he was putting God first. Mike Pence, even though he had been part of the Washington political system before as US House of Representatives for the State of Indiana in 2003 after serving in that capacity to run for governor in the State of Indiana, can be considered as an outsider who made up the Trump team even though he experienced about how things run in Washington DC. That quality gave him more chances of being a candidate of Trump's choice. The Republicans hoped to use Mike Pence for negotiation and his bipartism skills to pass some key legislative policies together with the democratic members.

Fast forward to the present, Mike Pence has turned out to be a very quality picked vice president. The whole world has seen him turn into a statesman for America and the highest Diplomat of the land, and this did not happen overnight. Mike Pence went through a process of serving people at an early stage of his career. Being a fine man and having a well-disciplined lifestyle which came from two source, a strong family value background will show how you were raised up by your parents. Secondly, it is one's moral value which came from the creator which Mike Pence emulates in his daily life. I hope we all emulate such lifestyle which brings no condemnation because of a well-disciplined way of life.

CHAPTER 6

A Leap of Faith by Mike Pence

Did Mike Pence receive a confirmation from God to join the Trump team? As a Christian, it takes great faith to make such move that Mike Pence did in accepting Trump's call as the selected running mate for the 2016 election. Remember, Mike Pence was about or already started to put his campaign together for governorship of the State of Indiana. Putting one's campaign to an end and taking up another which is for a higher call sound like a form gamble and a big one too, knowing the huge amount of controversies that were already surrounding candidate Trump. Mike Pence accepting that nomination is not a one-man decision. As we know, he is married. He has to discuss it with his family, especially the wife because if they fail, they fail together.

In my first time living in America, I witnessed an election with one of the most controversial candidate ever. He was accused from all angles, including the Trump University scam, grabbing women's body parts, Mexico comment, and the list continues. With all these allegations, the Pence family still came on board. Their ticket must have been guided with some divine wisdom to make this choice, but again, some opportunities come in different package. Not all comes in a very smooth way. This is where your faith will be tested. It was this decision by Mike Pence that inspired me to write this book with all the fault of Donald Trump and cloud of controversies that surrounds him. This conservative governor with clean record puts everything on the line, joined Donald J. Trump, and answered the call not only to Trump but to serve the nation. I am deeply touched. What about if everything would have gone down the drain? Time, money, and reputation are all on the line. But thank God for his grace. Also, God doesn't look for perfect people when he wants you for his work but always gives people with fault the chance to prove themselves.

With all these risks, Mike Pence joined Mr. Trump, and they hit the road to campaign together. The two of them together became a powerful force that many on the left under estimated. I have not met Mr. Pence in person, but what I have seen so far is, he has a very simple and quiet personality. He is not lousy. I also believe he doesn't like the spotlight, except for official purposes. One thing am sure of, he is an honorable and well-respected man among the conservatives. All eyes were on Mr. Pence. Why, I believe, he gives hope to many Christians around the country for a new direction of America. Many listened to Mr. Trump and the promise he made to the American people, but he did not give hope like the way many evangelicals trust the judgment of Mr. Pence.

Next I will be looking at what the duo bring to the table to give them victory that they desire. Mr. Mike Pence substitute the softer side of President Trump. In my own opinion, it is like a union of a couple—a wife and a husband. One of them is gentle and calm while the other is a loud mouth, a disruptor. How does this type of union last without one lashing out at the other? Or worst case scenario, they go separate ways. What I found amazing about the two is that they have few things in common. As I spoke about the background of Mr. Pence previously about his work ethics and family background, being hardworking and ready to serve their country, I see this in both of them. But the main value or asset that Mike Pence brought to this team is that of his experience as a governor which gave him executive knowledge. Also, he was once a US congressman and knows how Washington DC operates.

Being a governor is like running a small country. If you have all such experience pack down, you can go a long way in pursing the role of a president or a vice president. Another major value Mr. Pence brought to the team is that of his conservative values that he holds so dearly not only in words but practically and literally. Pence is also known as a former governor who has a good track record of leadership under his belt. The state and direction of the country under the previous administration was at a tipping point to many Americans, especially the middle-class who felt that life has been shocked out of them by the rules and regulations of the Obama administration. I won't go too deep into what the Americans see in that era that made them want a real change. To conservatives, the bullying and silencing the voice of conservatives was on the rise. The mocking and provocation of Christians was also being noticed. Political correction was taking a foothold in the main stream. People were scared to name or call things as they were. These are some of the many things that gave the American people hope that the selection of former governor will help calm and stabilize the uneasiness of the American people. I give the RNC thumbs up for the brilliant pick as did with all the other suggested nominees for running mate. Whereas for President Trump, the moment I saw him walk down that elevator in the Trump Tower and announces his intension for running for president and the speech he gave during that announcement gave hope to many Americans. He called them *the silent majority*, but they were very loud during the election.

Candidate Trump, even though he is not one of the type of presidential candidate you have been used to, is of a different caliber. What the American people saw after he has laid his agenda if elected as president got many Americans excited and fired up because candidate Trump represented the death of political correctness in America. He began to call things as they are without fear of backlash or retribution by the public. He came with boldness and braveness that has never been seen before in a US presidential election campaign. Former candidate Trump's background is in business management and entrepreneurship and also in real-estate development; otherwise, a builder.

The American people were so sidelined that they needed someone with a different style of governing and not part of the DC *cartel* by Senator Ted Cruz. It was his favorite phrase during the campaign. Also, the American people desire someone who will fight for the interest of America at home and abroad, especially the fight against Islamic terrorism and problems caused by mass migration like what we see in Europe. Candidate Trump's agenda, which includes the revamping of the American economy, sounded good to the American people which he promised to deliver.

The other side to this merger is the opposite personality of Trump and Pence. Here, you have someone who has been a born again believer since his college days and has a strong family and conservative background put together with a New Yorker raised by a millionaire parent born in wealth well-known in media and entertainment, Hollywood, and the like which we all know does not produce anything close to a conservative lifestyle. Former candidate Trump was considered the life of the party in the entertainment world. Many rapper made references to billionaire Trump in their rap music, example phrase like, "Get rich like Trump." His background is totally different from the former governor Mike Pence, but the American people saw something in these two which gave them the courage to go their rallies to hear what they have to say and, boy, they did draw crowd. Over all, it was a perfect match because what game you decide to play, you must hope and wish to have good players in your team to give you a shot at winning. That's what I believe Mr. Pence is: he is the finest of the best. No bad report or evil report against the man.

CHAPTER 7

Do Not Be Equally Yoked Together with Unbelievers

A famous phrase or admonition by Paul, a converted disciple of Christ, to the church in Corinth at that time as he received message of compromises happening within the church among believers and unbeliever comingling together which is not good for their congregation because the church has to be an example in the midst of ungodliness and darkness. That is why Paul admonished the church as he had, encouraging them to follow the examples of Christ who is the role model of the church instead of following after pagan worshippers who don't have any regards or respect for their creator. Paul said in 2 Corinthians 6:14–15:

> Do not be equally yoke together with unbelievers, for what do righteousness and wickedness have in common? Or what fellowship can light have with darkness? What harmony is there between Christ and Belial or what does a believer have in common with and unbelieve?

I got the name of my book by this inspired word of Paul. We all witness the merger of two people with two different personalities and background as I wrote about it in the previous chapter. What played out before the American people in the 2016 election was a never-seen-before election run where all eyes were on these two people—former candidate Trump and former Governor Mike Pence.

After candidate Trump defeated seventeen people in the primary presidential election, everyone was looking forward to who his running mate was going to be after the RNC did what they have to do, and they came up with this fine, conservative man who has no trial or history of extra-marital affairs or public corruptions, except for some previous policies issues he had when he was a governor of the State Indiana. These controversial policies raised huge concern by some people in the left-wing of the Democratic Party. Other than that, he was clean and is still clean. This is a man who said he cannot go out to a public event without his wife because the world will always try to make up a story against you even if you don't have one just to destroy your career.

Moving forward, the main reason I was prompted to write this book is to focus on the reason why former Governor Mike Pence answered the call to candidate Trump, knowing all the baggage he carries along. He still accepted to be a running mate and did not push it off to someone else. Mr. Pence put everything on the line—his gubernatorial run and other opportunity to join the team in "Making America Great Again."

I compare Mr. Pence to a Christian that has all the moral characters including a good standing relationship with the Lord Jesus Christ. I believe someone else with such a good moral values and is a well-known conservative would have given a second thought to the idea of running together with candidate Trump due to his track record of being in the spotlight of media and entertainment. The most scary part of the then candidate Trump's life is the extra-marital affairs he had with other women plus serious allegations of sexual relationships he had with porn star and prostitutes and also a leaked tape that surfaced about Mr. Trump boasting about "how women will allow you to grab their private parts when you are rich and famous," a conversation he was having with then former ET host Billy Bush. That tape caused a huge rage among women during the primary and dragged on to the women's march in Washington DC.

All these allegations followed the then candidate Trump up until now. Considering all these issues behind or with the candidate elect, Mr. Pence did not back down in his support of join the team.

Another person that amazes me is the wife of the former governor because a decision like this to support someone as a president who does not have a good moral track record is incomprehensible for the wife to his husband. It is the green light. This is where I saw Mr. Pence going above and beyond to answer to the call of duty for his country. I did wonder where he got the courage and gut to join candidate Trump. That is why I stated earlier whether he received a confirmation from God through prayer, or his gut told him to join, or it was the right timing for America to experience a different form of presidency that has never been seen before, just as Paul warned the church of Corinth to not be equally yoked with unbelievers so that they will not destroy their good reputation even by hanging out with them.

Mr. Pence did not even let such teaching remind him to say no to the candidate elect due to the backlash him and his family will receive or the fear of candidate Trump losing because of his misdeeds or character in the past. Candidate Trump also said some things during his 2016 campaign that could have killed his campaign. We literally saw him surviving through something that other candidate could not come out of. The two was like a marriage vow between a wife and a husband in a for-better-or-for-worse situation they proceed. A lot of evangelicals had been praying for a long time for God to restore America once more in terms of law and order racial divide, security against terrorism, the economy, better Supreme Court judges, and for a strong protection of religious freedom. Even people around the world had been for America as they know that if America takes the lead in governing right, it does benefit the whole world. I was part of that prayer warrior team always praying for America as many us of did not like and approve the direction the country was heading for.

One thing about making prayers to the Almighty God is, we are free to make our prayer requests, but we do not determine how and when God will answer our prayers. I know many did not expect our prayers to be answered this way as many people struggle, even evangelicals to embrace the candidate elect. Even through their victory, there is still a divide within the evangelicals as to why so many embrace the now President Trump. They could not understand it. I know for sure that Mr. Pence is one of the reasons why many have hope in this administration as many sees this team as an answered prayer to many of the prayers that have gone up on behalf of this nation. Both men look like they are not the proper match, but they both march through victory after the American people delivered a surprising victory to candidate elect and former Governor Mike Pence that shocked the whole world and devastated the life of many left-wing Democrats and the old establishment Republicans, including the Never Trumpers. This takes me to Chapter 8. The American people were delivered through the grace of God over the candidate elect.

CHAPTER 8

Victory Delivered

On Tuesday November 8, 2016, the then candidate Trump who was the Republican nominee and vice-elect former Indiana Governor Mike Pence defeated the Democratic candidate Hillary Clinton and US Senator from Virginia Tim Kaine, who suffered a great defeat on the night of Super Tuesday. The whole world was watching patiently and anxiously at the same time. Many people had written off the then candidate Donald Trump, from Hollywood to Washington DC.

The optimism of the Hillary Clinton Camp also known as the Democratic Movement who had the backing of top donors globally, including billionaire George Soros, the acting President Barack Obama, and First Lady Michelle Obama is evident. I'm taking about heavy-weight political names including the most popular celebrities from Hollywood work their butts off to make sure Donald Trump did not get to the White House. I watched closely as the election results started pouring in that night. Candidates began to make some huge gain in the pricing of the vote. I was flipping through various networks as the votes came in slowly all the way late that night as the world watched.

Candidate Trump made great gains in highly contended states like Ohio, Pennsylvania, and Florida including the state Hillary Clinton neglected. Candidate Trump pounded those states heavily doing back-to-back campaigns. The Clinton camp began to get the signal that the night was going to be very long and disappointing. I noticed that CNN was taking too long to announce the state that Trump was winning, so I switched to Fox news. Then I realized Trump has almost won. The network was showing a split screen one for the Clinton camp and the other for the Trump camp. We can literally begin to see the disappointment. Their campaign staff and fans started crying knowing that the night was not going their way. It was a very sad day. Many regarded it as their whole world crumbling because the man that they hate and ridiculed and called all kind of names is going to be in the White House. Trump clinched the total number of delegates needed to become the president elect a total of 304 votes, and Hillary Clinton got 227 votes.

When the votes were all in for the night, it took Hillary Clinton a while for her to come out and speak to her audience. She did concede earlier, accepting candidate Trump's win. The Clinton camp was so ready that night to have a blast, hoping that they will win. But unfortunately, things went in favor of candidate Trump and Mike Pence. President elect Donald Trump and Vice President elect Mike Pence made their victory appearance that night. Each of them was with their spouses by their side including their children. It was great to watch as they waved and were cheered on by the Trump people, including campaign staffers who have been working hard on his team.

President Trump's victory sent a shock wave around the world because many people were confident about the victory of Hillary Clinton. I bet many campaign donors were disappointed that the money they spent did not gain any yield in terms of getting a victory that night. Vice President Mike Pence did not know that resistance against their administration will drag on to end of the first term of President Donald Trump. The personal attacks against anyone who support or work with the administration have been relentless coming from the left in collaboration with the mainstream media. These attacks range from shouting and bashing supporters, even running them out of restaurants in public places.

Back in 2016, Mike Pence went to watch the popular broad show Hamilton and was harassed by one of its members. Controversial things were said about him and his relationship to the current administration which has nothing to do with the show. Why can't someone just relax and enjoy a show without bringing politics into the mix? While Vice President Pence is most admired by many people, at the same time, he scared the hell out of many pro-gay and the LGBT community, but I don't see a reason why they should. We all have the right to our beliefs and personal moral stands on many issues, especially when it comes to family, marriage, and faith which are the basic and fundamental reason why America was established—for people to have the freedom to live and express their life the way they choose without infringing on someone else's rights. In a recent situation where the former vice president from the Obama administration, Joe Biden, said, "The fact of the matter is it was followed on by a guy who's a decent guy, our vice president, who stood before this group of allies and leaders and said, 'I'm here on behalf of President Trump,' and there was dead silence. Dead silence." And there went the attack on social media against Vice President Pence.

Honestly speaking, the man is a decent man—a family man who respects his wife, loves his country, and is a man of faith and does not shy away from his belief which is an attitude that has not been seen for a very long time in a politician. Because Biden called him decent, the liberal left pounced back. Example, on Twitter, Cynthia Nixon, an actress and was once a candidate in the state of New York running for governor but failed to pull it off, tweeted, "@JoeBiden, you have just called America's most anti-LGBT elected leader a decent guy. Please consider how this falls on the ears of our community."

Because of the politically correct world we live in, the former vice president quickly issued an apology to Cynthia Nixon. Biden wrote, "I was making a point on a world stage in a foreign policy context that under normal circumstance, a vice president wouldn't be given a silent reaction on the world stage," he said. "But there is nothing decent being anti-LGBTQ rights, and that includes the vice president."

"On another occasion on the popular show *The View*, one of the host member made a mockery of Vice President Mike Pence about his Christian faith. If anyone knows something about Christians, they know that evangelical Christians strongly believe in having a relationship with Jesus Christ. That includes communicating with him through prayers. In a segment on the show called *The View*, co-host Joy Behar did take a shot at Vice President Mike Pence's Christian faith, saying that talking to Jesus is one thing, but hearing Jesus talk back to you could be described as *mental illness*. This whole thing started when the White House staffer and former apprentice star Omarosa was discussing how uncomfortable she felt around Pence.

"As bad as you think Trump is, you would worried about Pence everyone that is wishing for Trump to be impeach might want to reconsider their life." She said that on the celebrity *Big Brother* show that was on that time. "I am a Christian. I love Jesus, but he thinks Jesus tells him to say things." That is when Joy Behar said what she said about Trump.

Me personally, I do not watch *The View*. It seemed, to me, like bunch of women screaming and yelling at each other and getting paid millions of dollars to do nothing, how sweet America is. These personal attacks against the VP has been forthcoming even when he was a governor in Indiana before he became vice president. I remember a cross section of the LGBTQ community in the Washington DC area put a protest up by the Observatory on Massachusetts Avenue North West DC. They showed their discontent for Mike Pence even before he moved to the city. What the left does to people who don't party with them or thinks like them is unbelievable. They will ridicule you and mock you, especially when you find yourself in public office. They found it very strange for someone to be in public office and still hold on to their values whether it is family value or faith value. They always forget about the right the constitution gives to each individual to have that liberty to live out their God-given right to worship and to embrace their family values.

CHAPTER 9

Is Mike Pence an Asset to the Administration?

Since Vice President Mike Pence came to office in January 2017, he has been one of Americas most admired statesman and has been representing the administration to the very best of his ability. He is a very stable individual who is qualified to represent the United States in foreign affairs and internal diplomacy. As I read and study about the background, the former governor has been a leader from his early days in high school up to college. He served in the city where he was raised. One thing that draws my attention is his consistency to push and pursue the things he wants in life, and he has long track record of always wanting to serve the public.

I was very happy and proud to see him serving in one of the highest capacity in the land, someone who has been groomed for this time. I want to say that the Republican committee or campaign committee that helped make Mike Pence the vice president elect made a very good pick even though then candidate Trump has to make the final decision. I am glad he called the right shot on this one. Vice President Pence made his first official trip Asia to attend the ASEAN Conference where he stopped by several Asian countries, taking the new administration message and agenda for the region in terms of economic and trade relations, foreign and diplomatic relations, and also military cooperation with the Asia Pacific region as China is trying to dominate the world and to send a strong message that America is standing in solidarity with anyone who is ready and willing to play by the rule. He humbly met with leaders of the Asian Pacific countries together with his wife, Mrs. Karen Pence.

The vice president has also visited other countries like Afghanistan and met the leader of that country which is a very difficult region because of the terrorist activity. He also made a visit to Cairo, Egypt, and spoke about those things that are very important to most Americans, like the persecution of Christians by the radical terrorists. The vice president has also made trips to Israel which is America's most trusted ally and friend, making sure that America and Israel stay as united more than ever. The Vice President also travelled to Warsaw, Poland. All his visits was to reassure that America's allies about our continuous support of global security and economic stability, including the global fight against the terrorist group ISIS. He did engage in major talks with other foreign counterparts.

Vice President Mike is a very strong and reliable leader. I consider him an asset to the Trump administration. When in Washington, he is like a silent or smooth operator that work in the background without making plenty of noise but, at the same time, getting things done. His domestic engagements include attending the Family Research Council Summit. He had also met with the Jewish community and also attends CPAC every year. Mike Pence is a well-known conservative who is able to rally up evangelicals to show up and vote. The vice president is always to show up to fulfill his agenda whether he shows up on TV to represent the administration or to show up late at night to cast that vote that will move the Trump agenda forward. He is ready to perform his duty. Some people in the political sphere have some doubt whether the vice president is loyal to his boss, President Donald J. Trump. Could it be that some are just speculating out of the blue, or they really want Mike Pence not to be loyal because of the huge cloud that surrounds the president?

I am not surprised that they keep having this discussion. I believe there is something about being ungrateful or disloyal that is not part of the vice president because you can look at the character of a person and follow their track record, and you're not able to link any of his disloyalty to that person or signs of disloyalty. Such thought never crossed my mind about the vice president. The vice president is determined to continue to work for the American people and the man that put him on the ticket to be vice president. Entering into their third year in office, his boss is becoming more *presidential*, referring to the mainstream media. They will both finish their first term on a very good standing.

As of March 10, 2019, the president's approval rating among Republicans jumped at a whapping 80 percent which indicates that voters are satisfied with the job of the president with all the investigation and presidential harassment going on by the Democrats. I consider the vice president an asset to the Trump administration because he brings a perfect balance to the table. We all will wait and see how they move forward with the 2020 message. The loyalty of Vice President Mike is not hidden while few people cast doubt whether Mr. Pence has his own political agenda for the 2020 election. I have no doubt the he will not be running for president with his former boss. One thing about loyalty is this: it comes with respect. They both go together. It's not that Vice President Mike Pence does not have his own leadership aspiration. He does have them because he has been that way for a long time. He is always looking for ways to serve, which is one of the many things I admire about him.

My speculation is, if he was going to run, he will not do it at this time out of respect for President Trump, which is the right thing to do. The Trump/Pence presidency, even though it got clouded with so many investigations and alleged crimes, have excelled beyond the expectation of so many people, especially by political pendent who think they know everything on what this administration will or will not accomplish. We have seen so many accomplishments in almost every sector of his administration, such as economically, militarily, foreign relations, and its policies. These include the historic job numbers since he came to office. This administration put together the best economic team to stir the country in the right direction and to counter the unfair economic practice of Chinese and other nations. With all these great accomplishments, why will Mr. Pence want to run a separate campaign for himself in 2020? I don't see that materializing.

Mr. Pence got all what it takes to be a president and to many conservatives and hopefully independent, he will stand a chance of winning a general election but will do this after he has finished serving the president. I write this with great confidence because of the moral standing of Mr. Pence. Doing something like that will go against his conscience and will not play well with the conservative base and many die-hard patriot out there because it will be a huge distraction. I believe there are greater accomplishments that await the president and Vice President Pence if they get to serve for the second term. So to all those whisperers or gossipers out there who can't wait for him to betray the president, sorry to tell you, that's not going to the happen. Mr. Pence is as an asset to this administration as he plays a major role in linking the bridge with evangelicals for Trump even though President Trump has built his own personal relationship with the evangelicals by delivering on the promises and by being a man of his word. Some people in the mainstream media just had a wishful thinking that Mr. Pence might not run again with President Trump because of all the challenges the administration faces and by the attacks coming from the other side of the isle. I still believe Mr. Pence is with president to the end of his term, win or lose. But hopefully, they are heading for a second win that will have some kind of tranquility compared to his first term in office.

CHAPTER 10

The Release of Mueller Report

Since the Robert Mueller report came out at the time when I am wrapping up writing my book. I had to include this as part of the story because this investigation has been hovering over this administration for over two years with endless allegation and distraction for the administration.

On March 22, 2019, the long-awaited conclusion of the Mueller report was released to the new Attorney General William Barr and was later presented to Congress. The Russian investigation has the country deeply divided because of the narrative of the mainstream media and how they made the Trump-Russia story an everyday headline news. Networks such as CNN, MSNBC, ABC, PBS, and a host of other media outlets, together with their host and news anchors, stood by that allegation as if it were true. The sad part of it is that even former intelligent officials will go on with these networks repeatedly stating that President Trump and his team have been working with the Russians and also stole the election from Hillary Clinton. Many Americans including me did not buy into the narrative because in November 2016, there were no Russians at the polling stations around the country.

It was people like me who voted twice for President Barack Obama and decided to vote to a different candidate even though so many people label both presidential nominee less of two evil, so voters were in a very tight spot about who to vote for. We had Hillary who has been in the political arena for years plus her record as secretary of state and the setting up of private e-mail server in her house which doesn't sound right and is against the law, so we have someone who will do anything she wants without thinking about the effect and someone who is a businessman and famous TV personality who has been accused of several misdeed such as cheating and sleeping with prostitute and was also accused that he will bankrupt America just like he bankrupted his casinos and business. All these allegations were brought forward, like the Trump University etc. There were too many things people needed to dig through to make a final decision, but the American people voted their conscience just as Senator Ted Cruz encouraged his base to vote. The people voted and elected President Trump. Well, it did not go well with members of the previous administration and some higher ups at the DOJ.

That's how the birth of the Russian story began just because Hillary Clinton lost the election to Donald Trump. The Democratic Party and all its members with the bitterness of losing to Donald Trump seized on the Russia story as their last resort in removing President Trump out of office. The president has said it over that it was a witch hunt and a hoax. He stood by his instinct.

The Democrats, after winning the 2018 primary election season, were very much determined to go all in on President Trump from all areas of his life with investigation. Even though the Mueller investigation has indicted several of the president's associates, none of the indictment were related to Russian collusion. One thing I noticed about the left-wing media whenever they are presenting their case or new to their audience is, they will never distinguish the difference in the indictment of President Trump's associate from their personal entanglement in their private business and the Trump campaign. They blankly state that the Mueller investigation has indicted over thirty people including his personal attorney, Michael Cohen.

I bet they will never mention that they are not related to the campaign even though they work for the president. The Democrats also tried to push legislation that will protect the Mueller investigation as all of them hope that that will be their final arsenal, lol. But Senate majority leader Mitch McConnell was adamant and refused to accept such legislation to the floor, assuring Democrats that the investigation will not be tampered with even the president and also gave assurance that he will let the Mueller investigation play itself out but still call it witch hunt which he stood by.

It is a bit ironic to the same Mueller that the Democrats were protecting and cherishing like precious but has now become a thorn in their flesh. Some are saying Mueller might have been compromised. They are calling the final report a false report and that it is not legit that they still believe President Trump colluded with Russians and also obstructed justice by firing former FBI director James Comey, but the man they were hoping that will give them that silver bullet has put their expectation in disbelief. According to Mueller report, there will not be any more indictment in the investigation and that the president did not obstruct justice and no collusion charges will be filed against him which is the opposite of what the Democrats were expecting from Robert Mueller. When the news broke out on Friday, March 23, the left-wing media had some serious meltdown. It was like election night all over again.

The Mueller report did not come out the way the Democrats were expecting it. In fact, many sees it as a huge present to President Trump and a big win as many Democrat congressmen and women are still at rage about the 2020 presidential hopefuls and still hold on to the Russian hoax. Some even say they will take the matter all the way to the Supreme Court to indict the president which is laughable. Sometimes, I wonder where these elected officials got their law degrees from. A professor of law, Alan Dershowitz, an American constitution lawyer and a professor at Harvard law have spoken on TV shows since this investigation started that Mueller had no basis of finding the president guilty of wrongdoing.

Shaun Hannity of Fox News, one of the president's earliest supporter when everyone else was afraid to speak boldly in support of Trump, has been pointing out the flaws in the allegation against the president. But all of that fell in deaf ears of the Democrats and the left-wing media. Some of them even indict the president way before the Mueller report. People such as Maxine Water has become a forever laughing stock because of her nonstop screaming and yelling about the president colluding with Russia. Now that the president has been exonerated, I was wondering if they will bow their head in shame and apologize to the American people together with the mainstream media, but I saw that coming.

In this administration, we have seen the lows and the high. I really admire the courage of the president throughout this whole audile which has made the president stronger, and I believe with the cloud now over the administration is about to enjoy more victories in accomplishing the mission for which he was elected for. I also appreciate Mike Pence's courage which, I know, they themselves knew all along that it was a lie and that it was all made to illegally remove a duly elected president from office. I, personally, am glad that this is over and hope that the Democrats and the media will honestly seek the interest of the American people, but it seems that we cannot rely on the media to be our voice anymore as they have destroyed their reputation for good.

Summary

In summary, I am very excited. I am already at the end of this book. Even though it's ten chapters, I hope it will shed a light on the journey of our current vice president from his birthplace in Indiana. His brief life history from college to his faith and his determination to serve in public office which a lot people shy away from.

I see him personally in my own view that he was born to serve and lead, and destiny is something you can't shy away from or else, your joy will not be fulfilled. This book also gives the challenges he faces while serving in public office and have been balancing to live out his faith without caving in to pressures from a secularist society and still be effective in his duties as a public servant.

As I was doing my research on some of Mr. Pence's policies, I came across a blog article written by McKay Coppins from the *Atlantic*. I'm not sure if they are media outlet or just a news blog. In his writing, he was portraying Mr. Pence as "a man serving two masters." That is, him being a dedicated Christian and a public servant at the same time. It was kind of a conflict of interest between Mr. Pence and his faith. What this writer projects in his writing is what has been preventing a lot of Christians from participating in public office, fearful of not having a balance between their faith and their public practice or executing government policies forgetting that the founding fathers made provision in the constitution that you can still cling to your faith and serve in public office, for it is not an abomination as long as you do what you preach and not self-destruct by compromising yourself.

This book also gives a detail of the risk Mr. Pence took in to run as a vice for Mr. Trump that many people count out to not win the election as a huge number of people in the left-wing media and so many others concluded. This book also gives their victory story and talks about the attacks on Mike Pence because of his religious views. You will also read about the "cloud" over the administration and how the Release of the Mueller report relieved the administration and the country as whole from the Russian hoax and millions of taxpayers' dollars. Finally, you will read about his role in the administration and his loyalty to the president.

In conclusion, I want to thank all those that will purchase and read my book as I start my journey and look forward to writing many books on various topics and issues of the day. Also, I am very pleased to write about the vice president, a man who, among many politicians, caught my attention by his family values and his faith as an evangelical Christian. Before, I thought that if you are a dedicated Christian, you should not be involved in politics, but I had it all wrong. He displayed an example that shows that Christians need to get involved in government instead of not doing anything. It has really been an eye-opener for me personally as we see so many people suffering around the world because of bad governance and poor decision of leaders. I hope this encourages many other people, especially the young and coming generation who have a passion for serving people with honesty and not for selfish gain which is a noble act to engage on.

At this point, I want to thank God Almighty for giving me the ability to write and put this book together—something that started with a dream that I have before the end of the 2016 election. The dream I had was very strange. It went like this:

In the dream, I found something that I cannot specifically remember, but the thing I found belongs to the president, and I presented the missing item and was rewarded few months later. The idea came to me to write a book about Mr. Pence, and the title came to me also, which is *Mike Pence: Equally Yoked by Grace*, a common phrase known to the Christian community.

Even though Mr. Pence is not the president, but he is the vice president. And what I wrote about is about him his life and journey so it belongs to him. I hope this explains the meaning of the dream because God given dreams to people before that have changed their lives for good. I hope to be one God bless you all, God bless our president, God bless the vice president and family, Finally God bless this great country the United States of America.

ABOUT THE AUTHOR

My name is Alfred Stephen Kanu. I was born and raised in a small town called Gloucester village in Sierra Leone, West Africa, a nation colonized by British. I lived and grew up there until I was twenty-three years of age. When God gave me the privilege to travel to the United States as a legal, permanent resident with the benefit of becoming a US citizen after five years with unhindered background or criminal records and by God's grace after five years, I became a naturalized US citizen and a patriotic one too. I will not be going too deep about myself or my biography. I will leave that for another writing opportunity.

Currently, I live in small city in Maryland for the past fifteen years. I am blessed to be married to a beautiful woman, Jennifer Kanu. Through her, God has blessed us with three beautiful kids—Alexander, the oldest; Abigail, my daughter and the middle child; and last but not the least, Alfred Junior. Before I move further, I would like you all to know that I am a practicing Christian. I guess most of you can tell by now with my many references to God and his blessing to me. Just to let you know, I am a first-time writer and I do not hold any political position. I am not a professional writer, but I hope after this, I will become one. The only thing I can say is, living in America for the past fifteen years has made me develop some interest in American politics and its system of government.

CPSIA information can be obtained
at www.ICGtesting.com
Printed in the USA
BVHW031733010323
R14708400001B/R147084PG659392BVX00001B/1

9 781098 004262